Mentoring My Elementary-and Middle-School Students to Become Powerful Navigators of Success

Mentoring My Elementary-and Middle-School Students to Become Powerful Navigators of Success

An Interactive Handbook for Teachers and Students in Grades Two to Eight

Todd Jason Feltman, PhD

ISBN: 1548719617
ISBN 13: 9781548719616

This handbook is in memory of my **four incredible grandparents and one amazing uncle** who could not be with me to witness this publication. Thank you for providing me with an internal push of determination and believing in me. I love and miss the five of you.

This handbook is in honor of—

The teachers, coaches, paraprofessionals, parent coordinators, school personnel, principals, assistant principals, network colleagues, and superintendents with whom I have worked. You make learning real and care for the well-being of students. It has been an amazing professional relationship. I learned so much from each of you!

All the students I taught: Every day, I learned from you, and I loved to see when you took charge of your education;

All the parents and family members who help their child(ren) take charge of their education and navigate success;

All my teachers and professors who made a major difference in my life;

My wonderful and supportive mom, dad, stepmother, stepfather, and brother, who are my heroes.

Contents

Acknowledgments

There have been amazing and supportive people who have helped me produce this second handbook. They deserve a handshake, hug, high five, and much applause.

My family has been a source of incredible support and inspiration. I could not have published this book without each of you. I truly want to thank **my mom, Arlene; my dad, Doug; my stepmother, Jeanne; and my stepfather, Alain,** for supporting me with my education and building my self-confidence. I love you all so much and am so proud of all that you've accomplished.

Mom, you've been incredible! I published my second book! Your vision and dedication to your successful businesses were a source of inspiration as I wrote this book. Thank you for pushing me to do my best. As a young boy, **Dad**, I will never forget those powerful words you shared with me: *a quitter never wins and a winner never quits*. I have carried this mantra throughout the years. Despite the obstacles, I never quit. I am thrilled I made it past Mile 20: The Wall. **Jeanne**, thank you for being an effective listener and a significant member of my cheering squad. **Alain**, your compassion and advice have guided me to write and publish this book. Your conscientious work ethic and attention to detail has positively impacted my educational and professional endeavors.

Alex, my super (whole not half brother), you've been a source of inspiration. It has been excellent watching you navigate and succeed in your education and social worlds from nursery school to adulthood.

Thank you to **Aunt Gayle, Uncle Stanley, Cousin Amy, David, Cousin Samantha, Cousin Alexandra, Aunt Dorey, Cousin Brian, Shelia, Cousin Kevin, Cousin Neal, Karen,** and **Aunt Lee** for your interest, support, and love.

Thanks to all the **prekindergarten, elementary-school, middle-school, undergraduate, and graduate students** who I have taught during the last nineteen years. Thanks to your enthusiasm, engagement, and curiosity, you constantly made teaching an amazing adventure!

You always let me know when a stretching break was necessary or how important it is to laugh. Thank you for inspiring me to write this second handbook.

Craig Palmer, a spectacular mentor, camp counselor, and lifelong friend. I met you when I was an eleven-year-old camper at Kamp Kohut, a sleep-away camp in Maine, and fortunately you became my bunk counselor and also my soccer instructor. Our friendship has lasted for over thirty years. Your clear direction in my writing and kind heart is invaluable! With your bountiful support, you went beyond the call of duty. Thank you so much, **Craig**!

Fran, wife of Craig, thanks for your support and being an amazing listener. Our everlasting friendship is magical.

Thank you to **Deb Eldridge, fantastic professor and dean,** for providing constructive feedback about my handbook.

Thanks to all my colleagues and friends who encouraged and supported me. You are amazing!

Thank you very much to **CreateSpace** for your fine work with editing, custom interior layout, cover design, and marketing. This handbook looks fantastic.

Introduction

Salutations!

Are you aware that school does not come with a set of student-friendly written instructions to help students navigate success?

* Are you an **elementary-** or **middle-school teacher**?
* Do you teach **second, third, fourth, fifth, sixth, seventh, or eighth grade?**
* Do your students know how to be **successful** in school?
* Do you have **disorganized** students?
* Do you have students who struggle to complete homework?
* Do you have students **who don't follow classroom and school rules** and **often get into trouble**?
* Do you have **students who don't get along with you**?
* Do you have students who **dislike** school?
* Would you like **110 student-friendly practical strategies** that will help your students navigate school success and take charge of their education?

Congratulations! You have taken responsibility by getting this interactive handbook and reading it. I wish I had received a handbook like this when I was an elementary- and middle-school student and teacher. It would have helped me tremendously. I want to provide you with the necessary strategies so that your students can become prepared, successful, and respectful individuals who take responsibility for their education.

As a result of reading these strategies, you will become knowledgeable in supporting your students with the following:

* **Preparation and Organization**
* **Successful Learning**
* **Positive Student-Teacher Relationships**
* **Behaving Appropriately, Respectfully, and Responsibly**

There are 110 strategies in this handbook. In each of the chapters, the strategies are grouped together by a common topic. Each strategy is followed by an explanation of the purpose to support your instruction and your students' curiosity. There are some **helpful reminders** throughout the handbook to guide you and your students. Some of the strategies have a brief checklist to support you and your students. I have used these strategies with actual students during my several years of teaching and within my current role as an assistant principal.

I have provided space on the page following each strategy in which you and your students can add an illustration and/or helpful notes if you choose to. Please share these strategies with your colleagues and school administrators. Instructing these strategies to your students will help you become an even better teacher. My hope is that these strategies will help your students become successful in the classroom and throughout their life. I am confident that their grades will improve after using these strategies.

The following suggestions are provided on how you can effectively use this handbook:

1. Read through the entirety of the handbook before sharing it with your students.
2. Select two strategies to teach your students each day.
3. You can teach the strategies in any order you select.
4. Model, practice, and review the strategies with your students.
5. You can photocopy the pages and distribute it to the students. The students can create a folder titled **Powerful Navigator of School Success** and the students can store the strategy pages in the folder.
6. You can always reread this handbook at any time to review strategies.

Good luck on a successful interactive journey with your students in helping them navigate success and take charge of their education. Your students will benefit from these strategies. Thank you for all you do on a daily basis to positively impact your students academically, psychologically, and physically.

Chapter 1

My students can be prepared and organized to have a successful day

Completing Homework

Strategy #1: Complete your homework shortly after you arrive home or during an after-school program.

Why: You will be prepared for the next school day. During the rest of the afternoon and evening, you will be able to participate in other activities.

Your Illustration and/or Helpful Notes

Strategy #2: Complete your homework in an area that is free from distractions.

Why: You should be able to concentrate and accomplish your homework at a quicker speed.

Your Illustration and/or Helpful Notes

Strategy #3: Take a few short breaks for walking, exercising, or drinking water during the completion of your homework.

Why: These breaks will provide an opportunity to recharge your brain to focus.

Your Illustration and/or Helpful Notes

Strategy #4: As you complete a homework assignment, cross it out in your homework notebook or planner.

Why: This technique forces you to be aware of what homework assignments you have completed thus far. This action can support you with organization.

Your Illustration and/or Helpful Notes

Strategy #5: After you finish your homework, put it in your book bag.

Why: You will be prepared for the next day, and you will have one less thing to do in the morning.

Helpful Reminder: After putting your homework in your book bag, **pack whatever you need (except refrigerated items) in your book bag for the next day.**

Your Illustration and/or Helpful Notes

Strategy #6: Make sure your homework is neatly done and handed in to your teacher without any wrinkles or food stains.

Why: You will be proud of your work, and your teacher won't be disappointed.

Your Illustration and/or Helpful Notes

Parent Signatures and Communication

Strategy #7: Have your parent(s) sign any school notes, graded tests, graded quizzes, or trip permission slips the same day you receive them. Then immediately put them in a folder and into your book bag.

Why: You will feel good about yourself, and you won't get into trouble.

Your Illustration and/or Helpful Notes

Strategy #8: Whenever you are required to bring home a school note, graded test, graded quiz, or trip permission slip to be signed by a parent, **make sure your parent signs it, not you**.

Why: It is best to be honest. Your parent has the right to know about your grades, behavior, and upcoming events and field trips. There is no choice in this matter.

Helpful Reminder: If you are caught signing any of these documents, you won't be trusted and will face consequences.

Your Illustration and/or Helpful Notes

Strategy #9: Whenever you see your report card, read it carefully and be prepared to discuss it with your parent.

Why: It is your job to know which subjects you are successful at and which one(s) you struggle with. You need to know why you received each grade. You must take responsibility for your learning in order to become a successful student. Your grades help determine what type of middle school, high school, and college you will attend.

Helpful Reminders: Whenever you discuss your report card with a parent, it is helpful to begin with your best grade(s). If you did not do as well or poorly in any of your subjects, explain to your parent what happened and how you will improve. You can also ask your parent(s) for help.

<u>Your Illustration and/or Helpful Notes</u>

Wall Calendar

Strategy #10: Post a wall calendar in your bedroom or on your refrigerator. Write down weekly and monthly assignment due dates, tests, field trips, and school events on the calendar using a marker. You should review the dates on the calendar every **morning, afternoon,** and **evening.**

Why: This will help you not to miss any assignment deadlines and to prepare for upcoming tests and events. You will become stronger with managing your time, which will be practical from now through your future career.

Helpful Reminder: You could use a different colored marker for each type of item to record—assignment due dates, tests, field trips, and school events.

Your Illustration and/or Helpful Notes

Sleep Routine

Strategy #11: Before you go to sleep, choose your clothes for the next school day and put them on a chair.

Why: It will save you time in the morning, since you will have one less decision to make.

Your Illustration and/or Helpful Notes

Strategy #12: Approximately fifteen minutes before you go to sleep, do a relaxing activity such as listening to music, journal writing, or reading.

Why: These activities should put you in a peaceful mood; therefore, you will sleep better.

Your Illustration and/or Helpful Notes

Strategy #13: Avoid going to sleep sad or angry. Speak to a friend or family member about what is bothering you.

Why: You will be able to fall asleep more easily, avoid nightmares, and wake up in a better mood.

Your Illustration and/or Helpful Notes

Strategy #14: Avoid using technology (television, Internet, video games, and texting) half an hour before you go to sleep (Petersen 2011).

Why: The melatonin levels (which help you fall and stay asleep) in your body will not be decreased (Petersen 2011). You should be able to fall asleep more quickly and remain asleep.

Your Illustration and/or Helpful Notes

Strategy #15: Set your alarm clock or ask your parent to wake you up fifteen minutes earlier than your normal wake-up time.

Why: You will have extra time in the morning to prepare yourself for the day. Waking up fifteen minutes earlier should prevent you from feeling rushed.

Your Illustration and/or Helpful Notes

Strategy #16: Sleep approximately nine to eleven hours each night (Petersen 2011; www. sleepforkids.org).

Why: Your body requires this quantity of daily sleep to handle all of the next day's academic, emotional, and physical challenges.

Your Illustration and/or Helpful Notes

Morning Routine

Strategy #17: Do at least fifteen minutes of stretching and exercising (jumping jacks, sit-ups, push-ups, and/or yoga, etc.) every morning.

Why: Stretching and exercises can wake up your body and brain and provide you energy for the day.

Your Illustration and/or Helpful Notes

Strategy #18: Take a shower every morning before going to school.

Why: The shower will wake you up. You will feel refreshed and clean for the school day ahead.

<u>Your Illustration and/or Helpful Notes</u>

Strategy #19: Eat a healthy breakfast at home or school.

Why: Your body needs food to provide you with energy to learn.

<u>**Your Illustration and/or Helpful Notes**</u>

Strategy #20: Drink at least one eight-ounce cup of water before the school day begins.

Why: You do not want to be thirsty in the morning. Water hydrates your body and is necessary for your well-being. Not drinking enough water can cause you physical and mental health problems (www.kids-not-drinking-enough-water-each-day-700291.html).

Helpful Reminder: Drink water during the school day even if you are not thirsty.

Your Illustration and/or Helpful Notes

Strategy #21: Arrive at school at least five minutes early every day.

Why: You do not want to miss any new learning, nor do you want your grades to decrease. When you walk into class late, it is a disruption to the teacher and other students. Being on time is very important for your education and future job.

Helpful Reminders: If you are late to class, make sure to quietly apologize to the teacher. You can politely ask your parent to bring you to school at least five minutes early.

Your Illustration and/or Helpful Notes

School Supplies

Strategy #22: Always carry at least **three sharpened pencils** in your book bag, or keep them in the back of your desk.

Why: You will never have to look for a pencil. You are taking charge of your education.

Helpful Reminder: Once you are finished using your pencil, put it in your book bag or the back of your desk.

☐ Do you have **three sharpened pencils** in your book bag or in the back of your desk?

Your Illustration and/or Helpful Notes

Strategy #23: You can purchase a different-colored folder for each subject (reading, writing, math, social studies, science, etc.).

Why: The color will help you locate a particular folder. Your assignments and handouts for a subject will be placed only in one folder.

Helpful Reminders: You must only put **subject-specific** handouts and assignments in the specific folder. Before you purchase the folders, check first with your teacher. Your teacher might request a particular color and type of folder.

<u>Your Illustration and/or Helpful Notes</u>

Strategy #24: One of your folders could be used to store your homework and parent notes. It should only be used for those two purposes. It must be brought back and forth from school to home and home to school.

Why: Storing homework and parent notes in one specific folder should help you be organized. You will be less stressed searching for missing papers. It is important not to lose your homework and parent notes because your grades will decrease, and you could get into trouble.

Your Illustration and/or Helpful Notes

Strategy #25: Purpose a separate colored notebook for each subject. **If possible, the color of the notebook and folder should match.**

Why: You will have a specific place to take notes and complete classwork for each subject. Your notes and classwork for a particular subject will be easy to locate.

Helpful Reminders: Make sure you only use the chosen notebook for each subject. If you don't have your notebook with you, you can use loose-leaf paper and later attach it to your notebook. Before you purchase the notebooks, check first with your teacher, because he or she might request a particular color and type of notebook.

Your Illustration and/or Helpful Notes

Storage of Personal Classroom Materials

Strategy #26: Keep your classroom materials in your desk, seat sack, or locker, organized and neat.

Why: You want to be able to find your books, notebooks, folders, and supplies quickly. You do not want to waste any time searching for your classroom materials.

Helpful Reminders: You can put your notebooks, folders, and supplies on one side of your desk or locker; and textbooks, workbooks, and your independent reading book on the other side. If your locker has a shelf, you also can use that.

❑ Are my classroom materials neat and organized?

Your Illustration and/or Helpful Notes

Personal Belongings and Organization

Strategy #27: Keep the inside of your book bag neat. Every day, you should clean out your book bag by deciding which items need to stay inside or be removed and what papers can be thrown out.

Why: You will become organized; therefore, you will lose less classwork and fewer homework assignments. You will become stronger in time management since you won't waste time looking for missing items.

Helpful Reminders: Ask your teacher(s) what you must keep and what you can throw out.

Your Illustration and/or Helpful Notes

Strategy #28: If you bring any money to school, keep it in your front pocket until you need it. If you have a wallet, you can use that.

Why: Your money will be safer in your front pocket and/or a wallet. If you take it out, it might get lost. You will avoid becoming frustrated over lost money.

Helpful Reminder: Whenever you wear sweat pants without a pocket zipper, you should keep your money in another safe spot.

Your Illustration and/or Helpful Notes

Strategy #29: It is better not to bring fidget spinners, toys, or electronics to school unless your teacher requests it. They can be a distraction to the other students and teachers.

Why: The fidget spinners, toys, and/or electronics could get lost, stolen, or taken away by the teacher. You need to be able to concentrate in your classroom and complete your work.

Your Illustration and/or Helpful Notes

Strategy #30: If you are allowed to bring a cellular phone to school, make sure to keep it in a safe place (your pocket or locker, or perhaps your teacher can lock it up).

Why: You do not want to lose your cell phone; therefore, you must take responsibility for your belongings. If you take it out during the school day without permission, your teacher might hold it for you.

Your Illustration and/or Helpful Notes

Strategy #31: If you bring a cell phone to school, make sure it is turned off.

Why: The ringing or vibration tone will distract you, the other students, and your teachers.

❏ Did I remember to turn off my cell phone?

Your Illustration and/or Helpful Notes

Lock and Locker

Strategy #32: If you have a locker, practice opening your combination or key lock several times before the school year begins.

Why: You will feel confident that you can open your locker even when you are in a rush. Mastering this important skill will prevent you from being late to class.

Helpful Reminders: Write down your locker combination on a piece of paper, and keep it at home. At the beginning of the school year, you should also keep a copy of your combination in your pocket in case you need it.

☐ Have I **practiced opening my combination or key lock *at least ten times*?**

☐ Can I **open my combination or key lock in under *twenty seconds*?**

Your Illustration and/or Helpful Notes

Strategy #33: Don't share your lock combination or key with any of your friends. You, your parent, and a teacher or assistant principal are the only ones who should know the combination and/or have a duplicate key.

Why: Your locker contains your belongings. You do not want any of your belongings to go missing either by mistake or on purpose.

Your Illustration and/or Helpful Notes

Fire Drill Safety

Strategy #34: At the beginning of the year, ask your teacher where you should report during a fire drill if you are not in the classroom.

Why: It is essential for you to be safe and to know where you should go in case of a fire drill. Planning ahead is important.

<u>Your Illustration and/or Helpful Notes</u>

Avoid Candy and Soda

Strategy #35: Avoid eating candy and drinking soda before and during the school day.

Why: The sugar from the candy and/or soda may cause you to act silly and not be able to focus. You could get into trouble for misbehaving.

Your Illustration and/or Helpful Notes

My Monthly Goals for the School Year

Strategy #36: Set a monthly goal in each of these three categories:

1. **Subject-Specific Goal**
   Example: I want to write fascinating introductions during social studies.

2. **Friendship Goal**
   Example: I would like to hang out with my school friends on weekends.

3. **Citizenship Goal (how you act and behave)**
   Example: Whenever another student is having a bad day, I would like to help him or her feel better.

Why: These monthly goals can help you make school exciting and encourage you to be responsible. They provide you with three categories to focus on during a month.

Helpful Reminders: Before setting your monthly goals, it would be helpful to watch President Obama's *Message for America's Students* (September 2009) on the Internet. Develop a plan on how to accomplish each goal. You can ask your teacher or parent for help. There is a document provided for each month for you to set your goals.

Your Illustration and/or Helpful Notes

My Monthly Goals for the School Year
Grade: _____

At the beginning of each month, you can write down your goals and plans in the space provided. At the end of the month, if you accomplished your goal, you can check it off.

September

Subject-Specific Goal

I will accomplish this goal by

☐ **Did I accomplish my goal during the month?**

Friendship Goal

I will accomplish this goal by

☐ **Did I accomplish my goal during the month?**

Citizenship Goal

I will accomplish this goal by

☐ **Did I accomplish my goal during the month?**

October

Subject-Specific Goal

I will accomplish this goal by

□ **Did I accomplish my goal during the month?**

Friendship Goal

I will accomplish this goal by

□ **Did I accomplish my goal during the month?**

Citizenship Goal

I will accomplish this goal by

□ **Did I accomplish my goal during the month?**

November

Subject-Specific Goal

I will accomplish this goal by

☐ **Did I accomplish my goal during the month?**

Friendship Goal

I will accomplish this goal by

☐ **Did I accomplish my goal during the month?**

Citizenship Goal

I will accomplish this goal by

☐ **Did I accomplish my goal during the month?**

December

<u>Subject-Specific Goal</u>

I will accomplish this goal by

☐ **Did I accomplish my goal during the month?**

<u>Friendship Goal</u>

I will accomplish this goal by

☐ **Did I accomplish my goal during the month?**

<u>Citizenship Goal</u>

I will accomplish this goal by

☐ **Did I accomplish my goal during the month?**

January

Subject-Specific Goal

I will accomplish this goal by

☐ **Did I accomplish my goal during the month?**

Friendship Goal

I will accomplish this goal by

☐ **Did I accomplish my goal during the month?**

Citizenship Goal

I will accomplish this goal by

☐ **Did I accomplish my goal?**

February

Subject-Specific Goal

I will accomplish this goal by

☐ **Did I accomplish my goal during the month?**

Friendship Goal

I will accomplish this goal by

☐ **Did I accomplish my goal during the month?**

Citizenship Goal

I will accomplish this goal by

☐ **Did I accomplish my goal during the month?**

<u>March</u>

<u>Subject-Specific Goal</u>

I will accomplish this goal by

□ **Did I accomplish my goal during the month?**

<u>Friendship Goal</u>

I will accomplish this goal by

□ **Did I accomplish my goal during the month?**

<u>Citizenship Goal</u>

I will accomplish this goal by

□ **Did I accomplish my goal during the month?**

April

Subject-Specific Goal

I will accomplish this goal by

◻ **Did I accomplish my goal during the month?**

Friendship Goal

I will accomplish this goal by

◻ **Did I accomplish my goal during the month?**

Citizenship Goal

I will accomplish this goal by

◻ **Did I accomplish my goal during the month?**

May

Subject-Specific Goal

I will accomplish this goal by

☐ **Did I accomplish my goal during the month?**

Friendship Goal

I will accomplish this goal by

☐ **Did I accomplish my goal during the month?**

Citizenship Goal

I will accomplish this goal by

☐ **Did I accomplish my goal during the month?**

June

Subject-Specific Goal

I will accomplish this goal by

☐ **Did I accomplish my goal during the month?**

Friendship Goal

I will accomplish this goal by

☐ **Did I accomplish my goal during the month?**

Citizenship Goal

I will accomplish this goal by

☐ **Did I accomplish my goal during the month?**

Reflecting on Chapter 1

Which strategies did you find helpful and why?

Chapter 2

My students can be successful learners

Paying Attention

Strategy #37: Pay attention to your teacher.

Why: This is your job, and you do not want to get a poor grade. You become smarter when you pay attention.

<u>**Your Illustration and/or Helpful Notes**</u>

Strategy #38: Avoid daydreaming.

Why: You won't know how to complete your work.

Helpful Reminders: You could ask your teacher if you could sit in the front of the classroom. If you find yourself daydreaming, raise your hand and ask your teacher if you can stand up and stretch.

Your Illustration and/or Helpful Notes

Learning Styles

Strategy #39: Think about what type of learner you are in order to do your best.

Ask yourself**, how do I learn best?** I learn best by _____ (**choose one from Column 1**), so, therefore, I am a(n) _____ (**choose one from Column 2**) learner.

Column 1	Column 2
listening	auditory
speaking	verbal
seeing	visual
touching and creating	tactile
physically moving	kinesthetic

You might learn best in two or more learning styles.

Why: Once you know what type of learner you are, you can get better grades and learn more. You should tell your teacher how you learn best. That information will support him or her with providing better instruction to meet your needs.

Helpful Reminder: You should let your parent(s) know how you learn best.

Your Illustration and/or Helpful Notes

Engaged and Organized Classroom Participant

Strategy #40: Be an active participant, not a spectator, in the classroom. This means that you should be thinking, asking and answering questions, and using what you learned to complete assignments.

Why: As an active participant, school will be exciting because you are taking charge of your learning. Being a student is your full-time job. You need to focus on doing your best.

Your Illustration and/or Helpful Notes

Strategy #41: During any group or partner task, take a leadership role or be an active participant.

Why: You'll find the task to be interesting when you actively participate. Since you are leading and/or actively participating, the task should be completed more quickly.

Your Illustration and/or Helpful Notes

Strategy #42: Keep only the materials needed on your desk or table.

Why: You will be better able to pay attention and not become confused.

◻ Do I only have the materials I need for today's class on my desk or table?

Your Illustration and/or Helpful Notes

Strategy #43: Ask questions whenever you are curious or confused with any information. Don't be afraid to ask questions. It is likely that other students have the same question but are not asking it.

Why: In order to get good grades, it is your responsibility to understand what you are learning. If the information is unclear, you must ask so that you can know what is being taught.

<u>**Your Illustration and/or Helpful Notes**</u>

Strategy #44: It is acceptable to disagree with a statement made by a teacher, student, or within a text. You must provide evidence to back up your disagreement. Whenever you disagree, respect in your tone of voice and body language is required. There should be no insults of the teacher or another student.

Why: Respectfully disagreeing supported by evidence is an essential skill that students need. If you learn how to properly disagree in school, it should support you throughout your life and in your future job.

Your Illustration and/or Helpful Notes

Strategy #45: Whenever you are asked to provide feedback on another student's work, make sure to always begin with a specific compliment. Suggestions should be shared in a friendly tone of voice, never rudely or sarcastically.

Why: It is important for students to first hear what they did well in order to build their self-confidence. Then, they are better able to listen to a suggestion and implement it.

Your Illustration and/or Helpful Notes

Strategy #46: Always write the date and topic on all your class notes, handouts, and work you complete.

Why: When completing assignments and homework and studying for quizzes and tests, you will be organized and not waste time.

<u>Your Illustration and/or Helpful Notes</u>

Strategy #47: Ask your teacher to share helpful techniques on how to study for quizzes and tests.

Why: You want to score well in quizzes and tests. Now, when your teacher tells you to study for a quiz or test, you will know what to do.

Your Illustration and/or Helpful Notes

Understanding an Assignment

Strategy #48: Read the assignment or task description **_at least three times_** before you begin it.

Why: It is usually difficult to complete an assignment or task when you have read the description only once. Before you begin an assignment, it is important to understand what you need to do.

❑ Did I read the assignment or task description **_at least three times_** before I began it?

<u>Your Illustration and/or Helpful Notes</u>

Strategy #49: If you are confused with an assignment or task's description or requirements, ask the teacher to explain them. Don't be embarrassed to request help.

Why: You want to do an assignment or task correctly in order to receive a good grade. If you don't understand an assignment, most likely there are other students in the class who don't either.

Your Illustration and/or Helpful Notes

Reading and Vocabulary

Strategy #50: Keep an exciting book with you at all times during the school day.

Why: If you finish your work early and your teacher allows it, you can always read. Reading can be a magical experience.

Your Illustration and/or Helpful Notes

Strategy #51: Ask your teachers, principal, assistant principal, friends, classmates, and parent(s) for book recommendations.

Why: You might enjoy reading those books and have fascinating conversations with your teachers, friends, classmates, and parent(s).

Helpful Reminder: I highly recommend these two websites for finding great books:

* Popular Books for Boys: http://www.guysread.com

* Popular Books for Girls: http://www.amightygirl.com/books

Your Illustration and/or Helpful Notes

Strategy #52: Whenever you are reading a picture book, chapter book, or textbook, use an index card or bookmark as a tool for following along.

Why: It will help you pay attention to the text and keep you focused. Moving the index card or bookmark from **left to right** keeps your brain and fingers busy. It will prevent you from becoming distracted.

Helpful Reminder: If you don't have an index card, ask your teacher for one.

<u>**Your Illustration and/or Helpful Notes**</u>

Strategy #53: Whenever you closely read a fiction or nonfiction text that you are allowed to write on, make sure to annotate. You can annotate by doing any or all of the following:

* Underlining
* Highlighting
* Writing symbols
* Writing notes on the margin (the side of the paper)
* Writing questions on the margin (the side of the paper)

If you can't write directly on the text, you can use a notebook or sticky notes.

Why: You will be making connections and will be better able to locate text evidence to answer a question or complete a task.

Helpful Reminders: Whenever you closely read a text, you can use the following annotating symbols:

☑ = Agree
X = Disagree
! = Wow (surprises me)
? = Questions/wonderings
★ = I want to include in my life.

You can ask your teacher for other annotating symbols.

Your Illustration and/or Helpful Notes

Strategy #54: If you don't know what a word means during instruction, ask your teacher.

Why: You will know what that word means, and learning can become more interesting.

<u>Your Illustration and/or Helpful Notes</u>

Strategy #55: Whenever you are reading and don't know the meaning of a word, use any vocabulary strategy you were taught. The context-clue technique (reading the sentence with that word, the sentence before, and the sentence after) to figure out the unknown meaning can be useful.

Why: You will understand what you are reading, and it will help you get better grades.

Your Illustration and/or Helpful Notes

Strategy #56: Never give up on a difficult reading, class assignment, homework, quiz, or test. Be persistent and always try your best. My father taught me that a winner never quits and a quitter never wins.

Why: You will be proud of yourself and confident about facing future challenges.

Helpful Reminder: Ask for help from your teacher(s), classmates, friends, or parent(s).

Your Illustration and/or Helpful Notes

Writing

Strategy #57: Make an effort to write neatly. It can be difficult. Just do your best!

Why: It will be easier for you, your teacher, and your classmates to read your work. Neat handwriting can help you with studying.

Helpful Reminder: If you need help improving your manuscript handwriting or cursive writing, speak to your teacher, or you can ask your parent to purchase an inexpensive handwriting practice book.

Recommended Handwriting-Practice Book Titles:

Printing Practice Handwriting Workbook, by Speedy Publishing LLC

Handwriting Cursive Workbook, Grades 3 to 5, by Carson-Dellosa Publishing

<u>Your Illustration and/or Helpful Notes</u>

Strategy #58: Keep an ongoing idea list of interesting narrative, opinion/argumentative, and informative/explanatory writing topics in the back of your writing notebook. Whenever you have an idea, you can write it down.

Why: You will have ideas to write about and will not get stuck when you cannot come up with a writing topic. Writing can become enjoyable.

Helpful Reminder: You should request permission from your teacher before writing in the back of your notebook.

Your Illustration and/or Helpful Notes

Strategy #59: Whenever you are given a writing task, you can ask your teacher if you can draw your ideas first. Use your drawing to guide your writing.

Why: You might be a visual learner. The opportunity to draw first provides you with a plan to use when writing. It can support visual learners and/or reluctant (slow to get started) writers with producing detailed writing (Fletcher 2006).

Your Illustration and/or Helpful Notes

Strategy #60: Create a graphic organizer or outline before you begin a writing assignment. You can draw and/or write down your ideas on it.

Why: The graphic organizer or outline can help you earn a better grade on a writing assignment. It can support you with including all parts of the writing assignment in the draft.

Your Illustration and/or Helpful Notes

Strategy #61: Use a thesaurus to select synonyms (words that mean the same as another word) that are juicy and exciting to improve your writing and interest your reader.

Why: You will produce better and more fascinating writing.

Your Illustration and/or Helpful Notes

Strategy #62: Skip lines whenever you write a rough draft.

Why: You will be able to notice any edits that must be included in your final draft. It will be easier for your teacher to provide feedback on your draft. There will be space for you to make corrections. Peer editing will be easier to do.

Your Illustration and/or Helpful Notes

Strategy #63: Proofread any writing you do before showing it to your teacher or handing it in to be graded.

Why: As a result of proofreading your writing, there should be fewer mistakes, and you will receive a better grade.

Helpful Reminder: Don't show or turn in any writing that your parent would not approve of.

☐ Did I proofread my writing before showing it to my teacher?

Your Illustration and/or Helpful Notes

Strategy #64: Whenever you proofread a completed writing assignment, read it out loud to yourself at school or at home.

Why: As you read each sentence out loud, you will be better able to notice any necessary edits. When you silently read to yourself, it is more difficult to identify mistakes and/or ways to improve it.

Helpful Reminder: You can request permission to move to a quiet and semiprivate place in your classroom to read your writing out loud.

Your Illustration and/or Helpful Notes

Strategy #65: Whenever you are proofreading your draft, make any corrections using a blue, green, or red pen. During peer editing, your partner should also use one of those colored pens.

Why: Since these three colors are noticeable, you are more likely to include those revisions and edits in your final draft. Revisions and edits done in pencil or black pen are often hard to see.

Helpful Reminder: Ask permission from your teacher or parent before using different colored pens.

<u>**Your Illustration and/or Helpful Notes**</u>

Strategy #66: As you write or type your final draft, use a piece of paper folded in half, an index card, or a ruler to follow along the line you are copying from your rough draft.

Why: Most likely, you will not miss any revisions or edits; therefore, you will produce a stronger final draft.

<u>**Your Illustration and/or Helpful Notes**</u>

Strategy #67: Whenever you are typing a writing assignment on a computer, tablet, or cell phone, make sure to save the document after each new paragraph you write.

Why: You do not want to lose any of your writing and have to begin again.

Helpful Reminder: Choose a name for the saved file that you can easily remember.

<u>Your Illustration and/or Helpful Notes</u>

Strategy #68: After using spell check on the computer, make sure to double-check your final draft before handing it in.

Why: If you write a word that is spelled correctly but that is different than the word you planned to write, spell check will not catch it.

Helpful Reminder: After you double-check your document for any spelling errors, ask an adult to proofread your work for correct spelling.

<u>Your Illustration and/or Helpful Notes</u>

Strategy #69: Ask your teacher politely if he or she would be willing to review an almost-finished final draft of a writing assignment before you hand it in.

Why: Requesting feedback to improve a draft before the due date will help you receive a better grade on your final draft. You will also become a better writer.

Your Illustration and/or Helpful Notes

Mathematics

Strategy #70: If math manipulatives (objects) are available in the classroom, use them to help you.

Why: Math manipulatives can help you understand how to solve a math problem and therefore earn better grades.

<u>**Your Illustration and/or Helpful Notes**</u>

Strategy #71: Show all work whenever you are solving a math problem.

Why: You are more likely to follow the necessary steps. Your teacher will notice any errors you made in solving the problem. Since you will be showing your thinking process, you might receive partial credit even if the final answer is wrong.

Your Illustration and/or Helpful Notes

Learning Support

Strategy #72: Use all the charts, posters, and word walls hung in your classroom to support you with learning.

Why: These supports can help you do better in every subject.

Your Illustration and/or Helpful Notes

Strategy #73: Ask your teacher how a lesson will help you in the real world.

Why: If you understand how a lesson will help you outside of school, you may become more interested in a particular subject. School is preparation for your future career.

Your Illustration and/or Helpful Notes

Strategy #74: Make connections to what you learn in school to your life outside of school.

Why: Learning within and outside of school should become fascinating and useful.

<u>Your Illustration and/or Helpful Notes</u>

Strategy #75: Apply useful information learned in one subject to your other subjects.

Why: Whenever you make a connection to another subject, learning can become enjoyable and meaningful.

<u>Your Illustration and/or Helpful Notes</u>

Preparation for an Absence

Strategy #76: Write down the phone number and/or e-mail address of a trusted friend in your class to contact whenever you are absent. You will be able to find out what was taught and the homework assignment on that day.

Why: You will not have to make up as much missed work. You will be acting responsibly and preparing for a future career.

<u>Your Illustration and/or Helpful Notes</u>

In School Homework Preparation

Strategy #77: Write down every homework assignment and reminder in the same homework notebook or planner each day.

Why: Your homework grade will not decrease. You will be able to review reminders. Using the same homework notebook or planner will help you with organization.

Helpful Reminders: Carefully copy down your homework. Double-check that you have correctly written down everything.

<u>**Your Illustration and/or Helpful Notes**</u>

Strategy #78: Before you leave your classroom, carefully review your homework notebook or planner to make sure you take home any handouts, books, notebooks, or folders that you will need.

Why: You do not want to receive a poor grade or get into trouble. Being unprepared for any of your classes is not acceptable.

Helpful Reminders: It is your responsibility to put the necessary homework materials in your book bag. If you are a forgetful person, ask a friend or your teacher to remind you of what you must take home.

Your Illustration and/or Helpful Notes

Lunch and Recess

Strategy #79: Eat lunch every day.

Why: You need energy to pay attention and do your best in your classes.

Your Illustration and/or Helpful Notes

Strategy #80: During outdoor recess, make sure to run around, be active, and have fun.

Why: Recess is a break for you to recharge your brain and body for the rest of the day. Physical exercise helps you relieve stress and can energize you to complete the school day (Park 2012).

<u>**Your Illustration and/or Helpful Notes**</u>

Reflecting on Chapter 2

Which strategies did you find helpful and why?

Chapter 3

My students can develop a positive, respectful relationship with their teacher(s)

Getting to Know Your Teacher(s)

Strategy #81: Say "Good morning, (teacher's name)," or "Good afternoon, (teacher's name)," when you first see your teacher each morning and/or afternoon.

Why: You are showing your teacher that you are friendly and respectful and that you appreciate him or her.

Your Illustration and/or Helpful Notes

Strategy #82: If your teacher presents an exciting and enjoyable lesson, let him or her know that you enjoyed it.

Why: You will be proud of yourself for complimenting your teacher. You are reflecting on what you just learned. It will help your teacher with planning future lessons that will interest you.

Your Illustration and/or Helpful Notes

Strategy #83: Get to know the interests and hobbies of your teacher(s). Please remember that the goal of your teacher is to educate you, not to make your life difficult.

Why: You will feel more comfortable in his or her class and, therefore, will not dislike being with that teacher.

Helpful Reminder: You could also share your interests and hobbies with your teacher(s).

Your Illustration and/or Helpful Notes

Bad Day

Strategy #84: If you are having a bad day, inform your teacher(s) at the beginning of the class.

Why: Your teacher will be aware of your mood and can support you with having a better day.

Helpful Reminders: You can also tell the lunch/recess staff. Despite the type of day you are having, you are still expected to follow the classroom rules. If you're in a bad mood, you should not disrespect your teacher or the other students.

❑ Did I tell my teacher(s) and lunch/recess staff that I was having a bad day?

Your Illustration and/or Helpful Notes

Strategy #85: Whenever you have a problem at school, speak to your teacher first before you discuss it with your parent.

Why: Speaking to your teacher about it immediately provides you both with an opportunity to solve the problem right away so that it won't continue to bother you.

Your Illustration and/or Helpful Notes

Getting Along with Your Teacher(s)

Strategy #86: If you are having a disagreement with your teacher, ask to speak privately with him or her after class.

Why: Privately discussing a disagreement can help solve the problem without distractions.

Helpful Reminder: Calmly explain to your teacher what is upsetting you.

Your Illustration and/or Helpful Notes

Strategy #87: If you don't like a particular teacher, you should never treat him or her in a rude manner. Work hard and be an active participant in the class.

Why: You are not going to like everybody you meet in this world; therefore, you need to figure out how to get along. His or her job is to instruct you.

Helpful Reminder: You can ask for help with this situation from another teacher, your assistant principal, or your parent.

Your Illustration and/or Helpful Notes

Strategy #88: Don't make excuses for not completing your classwork or homework. Make sure to get it done by the due date.

Why: You will receive a poor grade and/or get into trouble. Your job is to do your work.

Your Illustration and/or Helpful Notes

Substitute Teacher

Strategy #89: Avoid disrespecting a substitute teacher. What if you were a substitute teacher? How would you want to be treated?

Why: If you choose to misbehave with a substitute teacher, you will get into trouble and be disappointed in yourself.

Helpful Reminders: Being a substitute teacher is one of the toughest jobs in education. If you don't behave well for the substitute teacher, you will upset your teacher.

Your Illustration and/or Helpful Notes

Sitting Up in Class

Strategy #90: Sit up straight (yet comfortably), and avoid putting your head on the desk.

Why: Sitting up straight helps you focus. Putting your head down on the desk during a lesson without permission is disrespectful.

Helpful Reminder: If you have a headache or don't feel well, let your teacher know.

Your Illustration and/or Helpful Notes

Dismissal Routine

Strategy #91: Wait for your teacher to dismiss you before packing up your book bag or standing up to leave.

Why: You might miss a learning opportunity or an important reminder that will affect your grade. It is a disruption to the teacher and other students.

Helpful Reminder: Your teacher is the one who dismisses the class—not you. It is inconsiderate to prepare to leave the classroom while the teacher is finishing the lesson.

Your Illustration and/or Helpful Notes

Avoid Leaving the Classroom without Permission

Strategy #92: Avoid leaving the classroom without permission.

Why: You will not be trusted, and you could get into trouble. Your teacher is responsible for your safety. If you walk out of your classroom without telling your teacher, you are creating unnecessary stress.

Helpful Reminder: If you feel frustrated or angry and need a quick walk and/or water break, raise your hand to request it.

<u>Your Illustration and/or Helpful Notes</u>

Reflecting on Chapter 3

Which strategies did you find helpful and why?

Chapter 4

My students can be well behaved and responsible

Following Classroom Rules and Directions

Strategy #93: Raise your hand and wait to be called on.

Why: You want to show your teacher that you want to speak. If you call out without permission, you are disturbing the teacher and other students.

Helpful Reminder: Whenever you have something you really want to share, write it down so that you won't forget it.

<u>Your Illustration and/or Helpful Notes</u>

Strategy #94: You should never talk while the teacher or another student is speaking.

Why: It is impolite and distracts the teacher and other students. Teachers must be able to teach without interruptions. Students can also learn from what their classmates say.

Helpful Reminder: If you are confused by what the teacher or another student said, raise your hand for an explanation instead of asking a classmate sitting near you.

<u>Your Illustration and/or Helpful Notes</u>

Strategy #95: You must remain in your seat unless you receive permission to get out of your seat.

Why: Remaining in your seat will help you be focused and safe.

Helpful Reminder: If you prefer to stand up during instruction, you should privately speak to your teacher.

Your Illustration and/or Helpful Notes

Strategy #96: Avoid joking around with your friends during instruction, independent, partner, and group work.

Why: You will get into trouble, and your grades will decrease. It will be difficult for the teacher to teach and for you and your classmates to learn.

Helpful Reminder: At lunch, during recess, and after school are more appropriate times to joke around with your friends.

<u>Your Illustration and/or Helpful Notes</u>

Strategy #97: You must follow the classroom rules even if you don't agree with them.

Why: If you don't follow the rules, you will get into trouble, and your grades will decrease. Rules are in place to help all students learn and not become distracted.

Helpful Reminders: You can ask your teacher to explain the purpose of each rule. You can request to share an idea for a new classroom rule.

Your Illustration and/or Helpful Notes

Strategy #98: Follow directions the first time they are given by the teacher.

Why: Teachers want to make each day of learning interesting, meaningful, and safe for you and your classmates. Following directions is essential for the smooth functioning of the classroom.

Your Illustration and/or Helpful Notes

Strategy #99: Keep all four legs of your chair on the ground.

Why: You might get injured if you and the chair fall down. Having even one leg of the chair off the ground is unsafe and a disruption to the learning environment.

Helpful Reminders: Avoid leaning back in your chair to protect yourself. Request to stand up for a few minutes if you feel the need to stretch your legs.

Your Illustration and/or Helpful Notes

Keeping Your Classroom Clean

Strategy #100: Do not leave garbage on the floor in your classroom.

Why: Your classroom will become messy, and it is not the custodian's job to clean up after your mess.

Helpful Reminder: Before you leave your classroom, check your area for any garbage on the floor. Throw out any garbage that belongs to you.

<u>Your Illustration and/or Helpful Notes</u>

Getting Along with Your Classmates

Strategy #101: If a classmate is bothering you, using a strong voice, tell him or her to stop specifically what he or she is doing. If that student does not listen to your request, let the teacher know.

Why: You are standing up for yourself. You have a right to be respected. Telling the teacher is not tattling; it is a technique to resolve a problem after speaking with that particular student.

Your Illustration and/or Helpful Notes

Strategy #102: Avoid teasing and laughing at somebody to make him or her feel embarrassed and angry.

Why: Teasing and laughing at another student are disrespectful and hurtful. These actions create conflict.

<u>Your Illustration and/or Helpful Notes</u>

Strategy #103: If another student is short, tall, skinny, overweight, weak, or of a different skin color, do not make fun of him or her.

Why: Teasing about a student's physical appearance is unfriendly. Please think about how you would feel if the teasing were happening to you.

Your Illustration and/or Helpful Notes

Strategy #104: If you are about to get into a physical fight with another student, you can say something such as this: "Let's discuss this. I don't want to get into trouble or be injured, and I don't think you do either."

Why: You are standing up for yourself through speaking. Settling conflicts through speaking does not make you look weak. Resolving an argument or disagreement using words is the most responsible and peaceful way to settle it. You don't want to physically harm yourself or another student.

Your Illustration and/or Helpful Notes

Strategy #105: Nobody should exclude another student from sitting next to him or her and/or from playing with him or her.

Why: It will hurt the feelings of that student. You have an opportunity to make a new friend.

Your Illustration and/or Helpful Notes

Strategy #106: Avoid telling secrets, including rumors about students or teachers.

Why: It is best to avoid this practice as it is unfriendly and can make other students and their teachers angry.

Helpful Reminder: Students and/or teachers might become nervous that the secret is about them.

Your Illustration and/or Helpful Notes

Strategy #107: Avoid passing notes in class.

Why: It is a distraction to instruction and learning. The note can hurt the feelings of a particular student, several students, or the teacher.

Helpful Reminder: If you are caught holding a note, the teacher might require you to read it out loud.

Your Illustration and/or Helpful Notes

Reporting Bullying

Strategy #108: As a bystander, if you witness any student(s) being verbally bullied, physically bullied, or cyberbullied, immediately report it to an adult. Explain in great detail what happened to that student and where the bullying took place.

Why: You will be proud of yourself because you are reporting bullying to protect students. You are taking charge of the situation.

Your Illustration and/or Helpful Notes

Going to the Nurse

Strategy #109: You should only go to the nurse if you really need it. Asking to go to the nurse to avoid doing work or because you're tired, bored, or grumpy is unacceptable.

Why: You will still have to do your work and solve your problem. The nurse will not be able to do anything for you. School nurses are hired to take care of students who are injured or not feeling well.

Helpful Reminder: If you are tired, bored, or frustrated about your schoolwork, or if you are just in a bad mood, speak to your teacher rather than ask to go to the nurse.

Your Illustration and/or Helpful Notes

Field Trip

Strategy #110: Whenever your class goes on a field trip, make sure to follow all rules, be respectful, and pay attention to the place you are visiting.

Why: It is an opportunity for you to leave the four walls of your school building and to participate in an exciting learning experience. You want to be invited to go on future class trips.

Your Illustration and/or Helpful Notes

Reflecting on Chapter 4

Which strategies did you find helpful and why?

Note from the Author

Congratulations on mentoring your students to become powerful navigators of school success!

Thank you for reading this handbook and using it with your students. I hope this handbook was fascinating and useful. As you try out these strategies, you should become a happier and more successful teacher. Some days at school might be frustrating. It is important to do your best each and every day. Please continue to share these strategies with your students, parents, colleagues, and administrators.

I am very happy to answer any of your questions and hear your suggestions. You can contact me at **www.toddfeltman.com**. Thank you for helping your students take charge of their education! I wish you plenty of success and happiness throughout your teaching profession and in life. **You are making a positive difference in this world!**

Successfully,

Todd Feltman

Todd Feltman, PhD

References

Fletcher, R. 2006. *Boy Writers: Reclaiming Their Voices*. Portland, ME: Stenhouse Publishers.

Park, A. 2012. "The Reason for Recess: Active Children May Do Better in School." *Time Magazine*, January 16, http://content.time.com/time/magazine/article/0,9171,2103732,00.html.

Petersen, A. 2011. "Grown-Up Problems Start at Bedtime." *Wall Street Journal*, July 18.

Sleep for Kids. (n.d.). *Teaching Kids the Importance of Sleep*. http://www.sleepforkids.org.

HealthDay. 2015. "U.S. Kids Not Drinking Enough Water Each Day," June 11, http://consumer.healthday.com/kids-health-information-23/child-development-news-124/u-s-kids-not-drinking-enough-water-each-day-700291.html.

Index

I
in school homework preparation strategies 92-93

J

K
keeping your classroom clean strategy 123

L
learning styles strategy 54
learning support strategies 87-90
lock and locker strategies 33-34
lunch and recess strategies 94-95

M
mathematics strategies 85-86
my monthly goals for the school year strategy 37-47
morning routine strategies 18-22

N

O

P
parent signatures and communication strategies 8-10
paying attention strategies 52-53
personal belongings and organization strategies 28-32
preparation for an absence strategy 91

Q

R
reading and vocabulary strategies 65-71
reporting bullying strategy 131

S
school supplies strategies 23-26
sitting up in class strategy 109
sleep routine strategies 12-17
storage of personal classroom materials strategy 27
substitute teacher strategy 108

T

U

understanding an assignment strategies 63-64

V

W

wall calendar strategy 11
writing strategies 72-84

X

Y

Z

About the Author

Todd Jason Feltman, PhD, has spent nineteen years working in the New York City public school system and local independent schools. He has been a classroom teacher, mentor, literacy coach, citywide literacy achievement coach, and assistant principal. Feltman believes passionately that it is a teacher's job to serve as a guide and mentor to young students.

Feltman has three master's degrees: one in childhood education, one in literary education, and one in school supervision and administration. He received his doctorate in urban education from the Graduate Center at the City University of New York.

Feltman is the author of *The Elementary and Middle School Student-Friendly Handbook to Navigating Success: You Need to Take Charge of Your Education* and now *Mentoring My Elementary- and Middle- School Students to Become Powerful Navigators of Success.*

Made in the USA
Middletown, DE
23 March 2021